Strange Life

Strange Life

Poems by Eleanor Lerman

Mayapple Press 2014

Published by   MAYAPPLE PRESS
362 Chestnut Hill Rd.
Woodstock, NY 12498
www.mayapplepress.com

ISBN 978-1-936419-35-7

Library of Congress Control Number: 2013958091

ACKNOWLEDGMENTS

The author is grateful to the Guggenheim Foundation, which supported the writing of this book.

"Bring Us the Last Nagual" and "Deadpan" were previously published in *Water~Stone Review*, 2008.
"Marfa Lights" was previously published in *Connotations*, October 2009.
"Sunday Brunch in Orange County" was previously published in *Milk and Honey: An Anthology of Lesbian-Jewish Poetry*, 2011.
"Gray Horses in a Green Landscape" was previously published in *Water~Stone Review*, 2011.
"Evolution," was previously published in *Water~Stone Review*, 2012.
"The Crab Nebula" and "You Still Look Good in a Hat" were previously published in the *Comstock Review*, vol. 26, 2012.
"At Night, the City" was previously published in *Pacific Review* (2013 Edition).
"In Her Other Life" was previously published in *Dark Matter*, Issue #3, Summer 2013.
"Dog Years" was previously published in *The Brainpan*, October 18, 2013.
"Grief" was previously published in *Bloom*, Vol 5, No. 1, Fall 2013.

Cover photo © Zastolskiy Victor/Shutterstock. Cover designed by Judith Kerman. Book designed and typeset by Amee Schmidt with titles in Candara and text in Goudy Old Style. Author photo courtesy of Jeff Tiedrich.

Contents

Metaphysics

Strange Life	5
Gray Horses in a Green Landscape	6
How Brief a Day	7
The Marfa Lights	8
Grief	10
When You Wake Up	11
Ask Ed About the Coral Castle	12
Bring Us the Last Nagual	14
We Made Art	15
The Nature and Attributes of God	16
The Moon So Loved Endymion	17
All the Influences	18
Matinee	19
The Glass of Wine	20
Sunday Brunch in Orange County	21
Horoscope	23
How It Was Foretold	24
Thinking	26
The Surfer's Way	27
Date Night in America	28

The Politics of Resistance

We Have Our Dogs and Their Ancestral Blessing	33
Handsome Stranger	34
Heartbreak	35
The Classics	36
The Next Age Will Be Enlightenment	37
The Fate of the Community	38
Anonymous	39
At Night, the City	40
Deadpan	41
We Have Trained the Jackals	42

The Faces in the Dark   44
Bread and Time   45
Leonard Cohen's Guitar   47

The Future Looms

Restless   51
Out of a Burning Shop   52
The Distance to Port Elizabeth   53
Here You Are   55
The Days of Joy   56
You Still Look Good in a Hat   57
In Kitty Kat Dresses   59
You are the Blonde at the Party   60
In Her Other Life   62
First with Splendor   63
Magic City   65
Dreamland   66
The Story of Tomorrow   68
By Nine A.M. You Are Expected   69
The Afterlife   70
The Eye of Horus   72
The Crab Nebula   73
Suburban Byways   74
Time Sits Heavily   76
The Girl of the Lonely Horizons   78
A Raincoat's Embrace   80
Little Girl, Little Boy   81
Evolution   82
Dog Years   83

Metaphysics

Strange Life

It's as if you are alone in a room
in an empty house and there's music
playing somewhere, the kind of
music that you always knew would
accompany a moment like this
The air is heavy. The water in
the pool outside looks like glass
The color of everything can be
described as *in the blue hour,*
which eventually fades to gray
Yes, it's a strange life
But wait. It's getting stranger still

Gray Horses in a Green Landscape

After the rain, on a rural road,
in an hour that has never come before—
That is how the dream always begins
And if the dreamer is a young girl
(meaning, the girl that we remember,
the dark-eyed one, always alone),
if she can make it past the abandoned houses
that have collapsed, like human faces dismantled
in last year's nightmare, then this will be her reward:
to see gray horses waiting in a green landscape
Two of them, the color of clouds
Immediately, the girl will recognize them
as the precursor to next year's spells
and all those that will follow afterwards
in the next year and the next

But women, women, surely we will recognize
there is only so long all this can go on
What has been dismantled remains in pieces
and even desire, as it dissembles, begins
to sink its teeth into something more mysterious,
whispers that now, it aches for no one's body;
now, it has no need to sleep. All it wants
is to watch as the horses live and die and
live again. To learn what their real names are
and what sustains them as the landscape
changes into a shining river. And later, when
the wind picks up, what they hear it say

How Brief a Day

How brief a day: this light, these breezes,
the lifted curtain, the window that looks
     out on the yard:

no one is there or ever will be
Morning, noon, and night go by
And then again. And then again

How brief a day: these glowing minutes
braceleting the hours, the hours like
a skin, a skein, thinning into memory
that evanesces in the moment that
     you turn away

It's just a thought: this light, these breezes:
     something to hold onto
The summer with its fruit and flowers,
the radio on the shelf, the old song

Just something to hold onto
because there is a darkness ahead
and it knows your name. It feels bad
about how hard you have struggled
     but it wants you anyway

It may let you have a taste, a morsel
before you cross from sun to shadow
It may allow one last look

And it will grieve with you,
but not for long, because you know
what it does, and why

and without mercy, you have
assisted in the process yourself,
learning from the very beginning
how to make your own tools
     to hammer it home

The Marfa Lights

Before she died,
this girl we knew said
Well, alright, at least
I got to see the Marfa Lights
because, in fact, she had

When we added that to her
farewell Facebook page,
we received messages of confusion
from as far away as the Yucatan

so we had to explain that in
West Texas, where this girl
was from, the earth sometimes
throws up balls of fiery light

that bounce around the sky
like big baby toys
or slide between the stars
with what many have said

is a marked resemblance
to the angry eyes of a
spirit lizard hungry to regain
what he has lost

Immediately, a thousand tweets
poured in: *Is that a sign?*
our community wondered
Should fear, confusion, rule the day?
But being who we are,

we already had an answer.
Of course not, we responded,
using not only the latest technology
but all the old, underground methods
that we love so well

8

A *sign* would mean "The next thing
you hear will be our instructions,"
and everybody knows that we
don't listen to those anymore

So it is our opinion
that the Marfa Lights should
instead be categorized as
a mere *phenomenon*

and out there in the dark and
troubled world, a billion, zillion
members of the community
passed on this sliver of enlightenment:

It's just Our Sponsor, doling out
more of those unexplained
interjections into the daily grind
that mean nothing to anyone

until you make the effort
to think about them
And dead or alive, we have
been thinking, long and hard

though we will not reveal
our conclusions until
the End of Times, which has
been scheduled repeatedly

and then canceled because
no one can imagine
what we would do
without each other

without these comings and
goings, and the little gasp
of recognition that is all
we are allowed to leave behind

Grief

Think. Is it because it seemed so easy for the beauties
      who got here first,
and now their journey from our wrecked and desperate coast
      is a story that's been scripted for the movies?
Because they write each other's names upon
      golden pages
and stay inside all afternoon, resting
      "in languid repose"?
True, the wind from the dry hills stirs the curtains,
but it's still a hot day because the sun feels like
      it has to serve these people
It thinks bitterly about their swimming pools

Is it because you once believed it would be possible
      to live here without work or money?
That old-fashioned queers would buy you drinks
in the holy name of how you used to be good looking
and share their medications because your grief has a
      name and size and number?
Because it can be seen from so far away?
That means nothing. Everyone suffers in this movie:
Civilizations rise and fall. It's all on tape

So think. Think hard. There must be something
      that you wanted, badly,
because you flew here in a plane, crossed each
      indivisible mile
with that creature of yours locked up in the hold

Or is it that you'll travel anywhere these days
just for the chance to set it free?

When You Wake Up

When you wake up alone and go downstairs
and the house is full of wind
and all the gates are open
it makes you wonder, doesn't it?

You may not even remember moving here,
to this house on something called the
Jubilee Parade Route, which may pass by
on a summer day, though that's a long time
to wait. Meanwhile, the grass is growing
The sun looks at you, then looks away

The chairs seem familiar, but whose
are they? The glass table, the ashtrays,
the ceramic figures—they are *reminiscent*,
which is as close as you can come to a word
that should be on the tip of your tongue
The air moves around you, ticking like a time bomb

That's right—look at the time!
A feeling arrives and closes in, suggesting that
you should be in the city, where you must belong,
on your way to see a client. So you put yourself
into that picture: up you go, in the elevator,
to the offices where men and women with
illuminated eyes are discussing things that
it appears they don't want you to hear
Go home, they tell you. Wherever that is

And suddenly, it occurs to you that all this
cannot be dismissed as the plot of a television
show you saw last night when you were drunk,
but it is also not like anything that you believe
you would have agreed to. About that, you are
absolutely correct. So pull up one of those chairs
Now, let us tell you more

Ask Ed About the Coral Castle

Listen, it happens to us all:
we wake up confused and sobbing,
chased into morning by bad dreams

while right outside,
the greenery responds to secret cycles;
crows on the fence share news about crows
Trains leave the station, food is slapped on
the griddle and people, hungry or not, partake
Where, you ask—*where do you fit in?*

Well, who knows?
If you haven't answered that question by now
it's probably okay, but you have to learn to
live with the uncertainty. Adjust, dear friend
Reorient. Never mind that the neighbors

are talking about you:
they're the kind of people who will criticize
your thinking as well as your housekeeping
Actually, most everybody is like that,

so you might as well start thinking
about the infinite (after all, in for a penny,
in for a pound). Think about satellites drifting out
of orbit, beeping *hello, hello* as they wander
through the starry void

or cast your thoughts down towards Homestead,
where Ed Leedskalnin built the Coral Castle:
one thousand tons of limestone gates and chairs
and walls and tables and no one has a clue
about how he pulled it off

Now perhaps you'd like to ask Ed
what *he* was thinking, but remember:

he only charged ten cents a tour so even
the poorest visitor could afford to be amazed

But that was Ed: in your little corner,
the rough nights continue, the replies
are hard to understand (if indeed,
they are replies at all) and as you may
have guessed, we have reached the
life-and-death phase of this business

so all suggestions are appreciated,
all theories will be entertained and
all ideas will be presented to the arbitrators
if and when any one of us
is able to discover who they are

Bring Us the Last Nagual

Ah, Carlos. The news about you lately
    is so disheartening
Just another sorcerer leaving on the bus,
    trailed by coyotes
A line of coyotes, marching on their
soft feet, stretching down the highway
    for miles
They are all that is left of the revolution,
of the bright days, the bright road to
    the infinite,
to our personal tomorrow: one energetic leap
    would fix it all
Sad to say how much we counted on you
Now we line the roads, we wave good-bye
The coyotes will be followed by so many crows
    that the sky will turn black
but not one of them will be able to
    look us in the eye

We Made Art

We did it! We made art. And it was easy
We slapped some things together, invented
a few others, and then carried them around the

parade grounds with our mojo working overtime
As a result, the soft brown mountains where
the spirits live wrote us a letter saying that

they felt even more magical than they had
in the old days, and then the earth gave back
a few species of extinct birds. After that,

all kinds of people sent us all kinds of things
to add to the art that we had made
You can look through the pile, if you like

We left it in New York City
on that summer day, in that room
with the windows open and the coffee

just made and the breezes entering the discussion
about the kind of final brushstroke it is always possible
they have yet to leave behind

The Nature and Attributes of God

It's not as if we didn't travel;
pack lightly, sleep lightly, in order
to pray in monkey temples and starve
with the best of our generation as we
brushed the speechless dust of the ashram
from our feet. The bloody sun
plunged into the rice field at the
end of the world, and it seemed
to mean something about the nature
and attributes of God. Maybe it did

And it's not as if we didn't confer
with the famous book of phrases,
even allow the words to marry and
unmarry us as long as incense was involved,
and the interpretation of dreams,
and velvet dresses. After all, that was
the world: accessible and cheaply purchased
If you said you were on The Trail of the Spirits,
soldiers would give you postcards
Dragons would let you pass

Now all that is left is just a room in
a town and a small boat that cannot sail
in bad weather. But on bright days,
it is still able to carry a passenger,
which means that until the last minute,
it is still possible to be grateful
The sun descends in glory;
the kindest words contain you

and on the postcards, there were only kisses
It doesn't matter that no one knows why

The Moon So Loved Endymion

The moon, climbing one night into the
pre-Christian sky, caught sight of that boy,
Endymion, and was touched by his humanity
That was always what got her into trouble:
she had an innocent heart. She loved too much
Everybody told her so

But she did like to show him off:
she took him to clubs, she bought him drinks
So what if she was older? She still
looked good for a woman who had to work
True, she didn't know who had employed her
but she trusted their judgment, except in
matters of romance: that was her department
and she had made her choice—that boy,
in all his moods and manners

Now they spend their time in the chilly suburbs
moving through the houses of the year
She feeds him stars. She buys him silver boats
to sail upon the lost rivers of his childhood,
though he is mistaken about that: there were
no rivers then. There were no pastimes, no play

But he is not exactly self-aware, Endymion:
at night, when the moon goes out
to light the eternal way, he wonders
how long he should expect all this to carry on
He's happy, all right, but thinks he could be happier,

which is what he tells his useless friends,
the same ones who howl the loudest
when the moon commands them
and will spend their lives thinking that
they are enchanted, when really this is
just another case of a woman with a problem
who still knows how to do her job

All the Influences

I don't understand how people live their lives
That is exactly what she is thinking, with her
dark hair and curry-colored eyes, as she
zips up everything into a nasty bag (that's right,
everything) as she rockets on down
to Virginia Beach where it is promised that
All Questions Will Be Answered. In fact,
she has business with the Sleeping Prophet,
or what's left of him: his institute, his readings,
his mineral baths, his cures. And if not—
If not what? You figure it out—if not,
she is going to buy a car with cool blue lights
and a thousand miles of empty road ahead,
and drive on out to the western lands
to howl with the skeletons. She is feeling
all the influences you are feeling right now
She is doing the driving for you. She is
willing to wait, but not a minute more

Matinee

This part is not about the movie: we are children
        leaving the theater late in the afternoon
This part is: a crack has appeared in the Great Rift Valley,
        stampeding the herds and emptying the oceans
From a distance—it is always *from a distance*—
        scientists grapple with the problem
but while a second moon is born, ejected from
        the damage,
one small blue planet has outsmarted them by
        saving itself

Now we progress to another scene: walking home
        from the theater,
the sky looks like it is on fire, but it always does,
        to the working class
In the kitchen, we eat cookies. In the living room,
        we watch cartoons

Later, you join the underground—fiendishly
        clever boy!—
and lead the movement to detect irregularities in
        the system
The rumor is, you have detected some. The conclusion
        is, no one is surprised

which suggests a theory about what goes on
        behind that dusty curtain:
maybe everything *does* lead to something,
        even if, in our current incarnation,
sometimes we never actually survive the flames

The Glass of Wine

The glass of wine on the table,
the table in the sunlit yard,
the secret animals in the shadows,
the creeks, the streams, the running rivers,
the open sea

The voyage to be taken,
the dream of a far shore,
the turning into the wind,
the wind that carries songbirds,
that bends the reeds in the lonely marshes,
that follows the meridians,
that folds the travelers' tents

has finally found you
with your arms spread wide
in your empty house
with its open windows

and the sunlight in the yard,
and your life, your life,
still as inexplicable as every hour that it lasted,
breathing in and out with the windy landscape,
trying, at last, to hold its ground

Sunday Brunch in Orange County

Huevos rancheros and mimosas at the
hardwood bar, just to set the scene
All the colors migrate, liquefy as we
get drunker. Football highlights turn
into angelfish that kiss us and swim away

Then there are the women's arms
wrapped in sliding silver—real silver,
silvery to look at, like manacles of money
And what did we talk about to pass the time?
The Christmas parade of yachts
and shopping trips to the Inland Empire
in a blue car. A beautiful car that
ate the miles like a magical bird might
eat the sky. A blue sky. Luscious. Alive

Who could pretend to regret a moment
of this? To understand that the time of
easy joy would pass? *Buddha's Dream,*
Healing Melodies: was it ever explained
to anyone that the channels we tuned in
 to hear this music would eventually learn to lie?

But they did. And now, in this dark haven
of dread, slouching beside some fanged revenant
who will have to pass for a friend, we are exposed
to the real deal, meaning, what we were born to want
in the hour of the deluge. How much, after all, can
one human being be expected to connect with others?
The manacles of love, the manacles of money
You wake up and they are broken
You wake up and no one speaks to you but God

Oh yes, Him. The sly Hebrew who is where
He is when He wants to be, except when
He is not. Today, He wants a drink

He wants a woman. He wants to love us all
and then vanish into the long blue sky
Reconciling His absence is all that we are
thinking about. Looking at your records
(the bar tab, the babes, the "accidental"
injuries), we're guessing that you are, too

Horoscope

In the law—not of Moses, perhaps, but of the now,
of the transition between the dark and light
of today—there is the principle of inevitable discovery,
which means that at some point, *you had to know*

and what you had to know is that your path
has always been the path of pain, not in the realm
of loss or failure but rather because it has been decided
(at a level to which you will never be given access)

that your job is to help others. What that leaves
you with is a life that cannot be completed through
interludes and incidents; instead, the idea

is that you must seek out lost souls on dead-end roads
and weep with them. Give them sandwiches, a blanket,
and a kiss on the lips. Within this context, it is ironic

that you wake up every morning longing to
fly off to the sun and beat upon its golden face
until your hands bleed—but what would be
the point? You have been assigned a house,
a duty to serve as a street saint, a good girl

And thus, no matter how bad you want to be,
you will have to wait until your sign and its
attendant planets have a conversation on your behalf

and then decide to give you something
that you really want. So spend some time now
and think about how, when you get it,

you will inevitably destroy it. Or else, grow up
and with some genuine mercy, take your
chances with the rest of us and let it live

How It Was Foretold

What they believed, the first travelers, was that
they would climb into the boat of a million years
and sail across the final horizon. Along the way,
they would have to answer questions, provide gifts
They would be expected to hunt with the jackals
        and at dawn, to eat a meal of grief

At the end of this journey, the Far Strider
with his belt of pyramids and diamonds
would tell them secrets. But if he did not think
they were enduring souls, then he would only
        tell them lies

They left instructions for how to follow them,
these ancient friends from before the generations,
but we do not follow because we think that everything
has changed. We posit that time itself is organized
differently and that the gods have congealed into a
solid mass that was long ago abandoned somewhere
        out on the blistering sands

But still, the great lion keeps his vigil; he keeps
his gaze fixed on the east, watching his own
image rise each morning, knowing that we will
be back. Knowing that the boats have to be
        unburied sometime

Because the journey must be taken—perhaps
when love lets go. When it finally folds its hands
and sighs, *enough*. And so it may be that no one
meets again, at least not until the lion finally arises
from his rock-hewn bed to prowl the earth,
searching for all that has been lost
        but not forever

What we never knew was how it was foretold
that always, he would remember us, and
that you—dreamer, born alone in stardust—
would be among the first to hear him
          call your name

Thinking

Sitting on the porch of a house in some rural enclave
with the sun scorching each green leaf,
      the thinker thinks
He is formulating the theory that human beings
may exist, in part, only to be interrupted:
that the smooth progress of their lives, their work,
      their dreams and desires
would not progress at all without someone
      walking in on them

In other words, it is the observation of the
human being at work, at play, that reminds them
      of what they are really doing
A person sees himself in someone else's eyes,
and what he sees (she sees) is the recognition
of value, the shock of perversion, or the sadness,
      sweet and singular,
in a troubled human's troubled sigh

After all, for all his life, the thinker has been
      interrupted
by women who want to discuss their problems,
by children who want him to make up games,
by pets who turn up unexpectedly in the kitchen
and want whatever it is, in their heart of hearts,
      they were created to want

But now the thinker has retreated to the lonely
woods and grassy mountains, deep in summer,
      possibly at the end of his life,
and having brought with him no women,
      no children,
no animals of any kind, he is simply waiting
He looks down the empty road and wonders

When the time comes, you will, too

The Surfer's Way

Even in the winter: to go
To completely enter the cold
and wait there, both in and above
the unknowable depth of water
(and all it contains) for the
arrival of a mystical force

Propulsion, perhaps, which we
have been taught to think of
as the act of moving forward
but of course, no one has yet
suggested to where, to what

But it is the surfer's way
to take the ride that breaks
itself upon the shore, as if
it is the tide line, changing

though it does with
the weather, the wind,
that marks the end of so many
hardships and wanderings

Day by day, the numbers grow:
those who believe this may be true

Date Night in America

It begins in the chilly morning
when the heat doesn't work
The alarm clock reaches out to you,
then shivers and forgets
Listen, someone whispers, *do you think
that the soul has a purpose in this world?*

Sometimes you do
Sometimes you do not
But either way, it is apparent
that the information you have
been given may all be based on lies

Indeed, this is the point at which
the familiar is going to be
presented to you as wreckage
so this is the point at which
you must open the eyes
that were installed and see
just how much has already
been shot to pieces by that
death ray you were issued
The one that says it regrets
its actions but adores what it
feels like to be good at its job

So it is you, my friend, wearing the
only hands you own, who will be
marched into the uncanny valley
and told that what you have to do is
just a little target practice, even as
you stand on the edge, in the darkness,
listening to the night crack open
with the sound of a vicious gong

But this is the point at which there is
no choice. So crouch low. Aim high
And wait for whatever lands,
steps out from behind the symbol
that represents the final sky
When it comes, it will be neither
dead nor alive. It will not be like
anything that you expected
In fact, at first it will play hard to get,
as if this was just like any other
date night in America

And it could be argued that it is
O dreamy dreams, O boys and girls
whom we have loved despite the hardship
and the pain, send us a message; reveal to us
when the scuttling lizard will become
the single symbol that represents infinity
and how we will know, when we need
to know, which way is the real way out

The Politics of Resistance

We Have Our Dogs and Their Ancestral Blessing

If tomorrow,
it turns out that our lives
are more mysterious than we thought
but our connection to each other deeper,

involving secrets about the creation of fire
and the folds of time that figure, mathematically,
into the distance between our encampment
and the distant stars, then even so

we believe that we are ready
More ready, probably, because we are friends
The scouts say it is dark up ahead
but we know how to live from meal to meal

We have our flags
We have our dogs and their ancestral blessing
Out on the road, we will survive the winter
In the spring, the wind will write its thoughts
upon the future

It thinks of us
It thinks that we will win

Handsome Stranger

Come, friend and foundling; come orphan of the storm:
we can go together into the dark woods
Not everything is just your dream, you know
Terrible things *will* happen, but you can
hack your way out of them if you have made
a study of how to—and guess who has

So come: we need a handsome stranger
We need all the perfect weapons that you built
from stars and shadows when you couldn't sleep
Come as the age you think you are,
the being you always imagined time would
make you, one who wouldn't even know how to die

Because what's going to happen has already been
happening to us: just listen for the sound
of the worm turning, the extra wheels being
slammed onto the powerful intentions with which
this time, we will be rolling into town

Heartbreak

It is not a hotel, though we thank you, boy,
for being the first to make the suggestion
We will take it up later, when the committee
meets again. But for now, we are still reviewing
the films that show how hard it was raining
those days at the festival fields where we were
a nation in the mud. Then the news came on
the radio: how everyone left their cars
on the New York State Thruway and
        wandered off to heaven

If this is where it was, then this must be
where it will be again. We know that
some of you have been thinking about that
since you shed your last skin. True, we aren't
getting any younger, but the weather
is bound to clear up soon. And remember,
        on the last day, they danced

The Classics

What can be made out of a gray sky?

Messages, perhaps: *things will clear up,*
or *all is doomed.* Probably the choice depends
on how a gesture of unrest passes from mood
to consciousness, because in the classical sense,
a collection of gestures can become the mood
of history, as in the things we did because
we felt like it, and for a time, all we felt
like doing was the directive for everything
we did. Which is why we left the place that
we called home, packing up our pieces,
summoning the movers and departing

as if we could reassemble any time: return
to the rooms in which we told our stories,
read our books. As if we could find our way
again along the avenues we walked with
real knowledge of the city and its fate—
at least, its fateful, heated love for us, and
how it listened to us until the interlopers came

but love remembers when at last, the
long-lost traveler calls its name (and we can
name it; don't be fooled). And it can arm itself
again, slip back into the streets. Which is how
we will signal to our friends, the ones who are
still in disguise, still thinking, planning,
sharing the classical sense that all skies are gray
before a reckoning. All days are numbered
All is forgiven—until we say that it is not

The Next Age Will Be Enlightenment

Who knows what it was we really saw
that spread itself across the lawn and in
the rooms; upon the days and nights
that no one owned but slowly went to our heads
Dreaming, we left the dogs to babysit the children,
but then, the dogs always loved the children
We loved everybody—probably too much

Oh yes, love, love, love: the old defiler
It drove the pretty girls into the movies,
the bad boys out to the land of the dead
The rest of us went into the factories
and came out humbled by our inability
to either use the methods of production
or destroy them. No: they used us instead
And they will find a way to use the children
if the dogs have not yet led them home

And where is that? the daily papers ask,
but why would we tell them? Already, they
have erected the day's beautiful blue canopy,
which often lies about its origins and purpose,
about where it goes at night and what it conceals
How hard it works to turn itself into sunlight for
our amusement and into shadow so we will sleep
All this, and we are meant to be appeased

But we are not. So now this has become
a story of survival. Thus, in the brief hours
that we are allowed to be awake, we whisper
to each other that the next age will be Enlightenment
and we are getting closer every minute
In the background, the plot thickens
Rumors spread. And one by one, the lights go on

The Fate of the Community

Out here, in the community,
we got up before dawn
and, holding hands with the vampires,
walked into town and gathered around
the loudspeakers, which were set up
near the diner. Everyone had coffee

A few blocks away, the ocean
—*our* ocean, our dear old friend—
had transformed itself into a sheet of glass
in the hope of deflecting cosmic rays,
or something of that nature
Its thoughts were turned inward
Deep in its briny depths, it embraced
its many secret creatures and held them close

Finally, the news came crackling in
over the wires that are plugged in somewhere
beyond the ends of the earth
Afterwards, we all agreed that what we heard
was not unexpected: at our age, where we live,
we had always anticipated that our medications
would be discontinued and even
the possibility of better outcomes denied

But that's only one side of the story:
in the other—which we are buying the rights to
with reward points—the factors that determine
the fate of the community will be voted on
by our demons, the ones among us, who already
own their share of the means of production
and in any future negotiations have already
agreed to testify on our behalf

Anonymous

The day the sun came mamboing in
      from the islands
dropping hints about having dated a guy
      who knew a guy, who knew a guy
who had seen the plans for allowing
certain alleged human beings to control
      the weather,
we exercised a little spiritual democracy
      and voted to get into the act

After all, we have always been "the other,"
neighbors out here in the outland,
where the morning flyovers rattle
      our little houses
and scare the pets—at least, that is
      what has been reported
In reality, we can read the messages
left by the contrails in our dear blue sky
      and we don't like them
We haven't liked them since the day
      that we were born,
which was not exactly when they told you,
      or where

In reality—such as it is—we have always
      been underestimated
Each of us has our own connections to
other types of (alleged) beings that we
      are not yet ready to reveal,
though we will admit to having hired
the Shadow of Time to shadow certain
major developments that soon may be
      reported on your TV
In other words, we are hot; we are here,
and eventually you'll get it: we are exactly
      what you need

At Night, the City

At night,
while the city paints its claws,
the sex slaves are still sent out
into the darkness to look for us
Oh, how we loved them,
every little monster
We even knew their real names

At night,
we can still hear the spikes
being driven into the ground,
the drinks being poured,
the come-ons being written
by the comedians who are kept
chained behind the bar

At night,
with all signals go,
the lipstick and the lingerie electrified,
it is tempting to forget that the city
once promised to stop lying

to those of us
who now consist primarily
of subtle forces
ranged around the outskirts,
knowing too much to think
that there would ever be
an easy way to get out of town

Deadpan

This is how to go to work: wear a coat
that you can hang up like everybody else
And that disturbing noise you make—
          stop it immediately
Wear your jewelry around your throat:
everyone will think it's just a necklace
Be productive but not inquisitive
Never claim to have stayed up late
But most importantly, keep a
deadpan expression on your face
          and the years will pass
Otherwise, as for the rest—well, they'd
never hire you, not with what you know

We Have Trained the Jackals

We are the people who are alive now,
but not for long, if you think about things
in terms of the big picture, which we do not
We have turned the big picture to the wall
In fact, we despise it for what it is:
a hallucination that clouds the mind of God
A joke He tells to His closest friends, who we
        suspect, by now, are all on drugs

Oh yes indeed, we are the people who are
alive now and we are investigating our options
Well, not all of us, but some. Our group,
for example, the hold-out community
who have just lost our leaders. We may have
eaten them, actually, or beaten them to a pulp
Or sent them over to the other side to find out
        what is really going on

In other words, we have categorically rejected
the neat little packages of time that were delivered
with the dry goods and the milk. In our view,
the ancient magicians—born and born again; mad,
merciless, hissing with rage—are the only ones
who should have tried to negotiate with us
It is the common attraction of their evil,
the extremes they went to just to decorate their
loneliness, that might once have persuaded us
        to cooperate

But those days are gone. We are the people who are
alive now and we intend to defy the era of
revelations, to nourish our anger about the years
of hard knocks. Think about the extremes that we have
gone to just to live this life. To last this long. By now,
we have made enough sandwiches to keep us going

until the next event horizon. We have trained the
jackals to attack at our command. We are busy doing
what we did yesterday and we will be doing
          the same things tomorrow

Explain, explain, if you still think you can

The Faces in the Dark

Didn't you hear the announcement?
Whatever you were doing, put it away
And go change your clothes: you can't
possibly be dressed appropriately
for the next set of events
that are going to be rolled out

What are they?
Suffice it to say that there is already
rain in the home counties, birds of prey
in the sky, and now everyone is thinking
that there will be days and days
of hard riding ahead

But that's why we called you
We believe that you've been ready for this
since your last sex-change operation,
since you built a better missile system,
since you beat the odds and
defied the state. In fact,

it is written, somewhere, that
you are exactly the kind of person
who would be voted most likely
to survive first contact

You, with your sub-atomic smile
and empty bankbook—where were you
going, anyway, that would have saved you
from the scheduled tomorrows?

So dress up, cool down, ride on:
just because the faces in the dark
say that they know what's going to happen
doesn't mean that you weren't born
to prove them wrong

Bread and Time

Being chained to the final floor
of a deserted tower
on a burning road
in a vanquished county
that has been stricken from
the maps has done nothing
to lessen the power of the
Persons of Final Becoming

They could be bound by a curse
to be buried beneath the shifting
sands and still be able to direct
your fate. There are six of them
or nine or twenty-seven, depending
on which story you believe,

how far back into prehistory
you are willing to follow the clues
But while you're asking rocks and
rivers to remember what they saw,
one day a boy will appear on the horizon,
armed by the Jews, eager for revenge

The sun will nod once in his direction
and women will perform the ritual of
cooking his final meal. Watch for him
on your little screens and in the clouds
that cover the morning. All we need

is for just one of us to admit that we
need help, the kind that comes with
a memory of the divine disguised as
a faithful dog who follows us across
the mountains, who is the love we
lived for, who lays down the law

Then we can break the world with
a hammer and all boys will be reborn,
all girls. Give them bread and time
and retell the story: the best one will be
about the day we knew enough to
start to cross the mountains and finally
recognize the truth about that dog

Leonard Cohen's Guitar

Yes, comrades, the future is upon us
Your tickets will soon be in the mail
for the kind of concert where you are
nailed to your seat, and then the aliens
arrive to announce the end of the world

But you seem like the kind of overlooked attraction
who might be able to make it out the back
When you slip into the cosmos, save one of
the little dogs and Leonard Cohen's guitar,
which, having composed the hallelujah

and undergone the transformation from tree
to plank to instrument, is changing still
Now it makes the kind of music that walks the roads
with a handsome mongrel, charming its way into
the record books and vowing never to give in

The Future Looms

Restless

Well yes, of course you used to sleep
a lot better when you were younger
We all did. And in fact, we could
conk out on just about anybody's couch,
or in a stairwell, or on the roof,
with the music of the future
playing the role of a summer night

But who led you to believe
it was always going to be like that?
The radio? If you check the summary
of events that have taken place so far
you'll note that it has already been arrested
several times for being a big fibber

and you can't believe the polls, either,
or the cultural indicators, or any version
of the Mayan calendar, or even cling to
the hope that because some stars may have
a secret companion; because human history
may not be linear; and because someday,
a heretofore unknown deep-space object

may intrude upon our consciousness,
we will eventually be freed from the
the limitations of our temporal existence
and be given irrefutable proof of
the existence of an immortal soul

Nope. The truth is that we've run out
of all the easy stuff and as a consequence,
you're going to be restless from here on out
Sleepless and aggrieved, you will wake up
every hour with the feeling that there
is something you should be doing

And you know what? You will be right

Out of a Burning Shop

Out of a burning shop on a cobbled square
emerges Mr. Aziz who is, of course,
a figment of your imagination—a kindly man,
and magical. A seer, in fact, who talks to the dead

which is just what you think you need
With your own life in flames, your future uncertain,
an hour of play time appeals: you picture Ouija boards
and levitation, but instead, he conjures up a tea shop
Are you aware, you ask, as you eat his cakes
and peppermints, *that your hair is on fire?*
That sparks are flying from your shoes?

At last he confesses to being an acquaintance of
your mother, an otherwise unknown woman
from an unknown land. It is she, he says,
who is setting all these fires, Heaven can't
restrain her, nor legions of imps, even telling lies

which is what you get, says your Aziz,
when life and death create a paradox:
a human being (and he means you)
who has no antecedents. A girl
without a history. A woman on her own

guided solely by the spirit of havoc,
which is, you think, encouraging—
even a reason to try again to be at least
some mother's daughter, dining by the light
of signal fires. While sending out messages
While hoping for replies

The Distance to Port Elizabeth

If you happen to notice, what you will see on the
horizon—which is currently displaying several
miles of choppy gray ocean—is a container ship
riding at anchor because it is too big to berth at its
destination, which is Port Elizabeth, New Jersey
If it comes too close, it will scrape the sea bottom,
already scarred by the wreckage of rusting
commerce, and likely compromise its own hull

Barges have been dispatched to help. Oil, cars,
possibly bananas—they will be floating back
and forth across your line of sight all day
While none of this seems poised to have
any direct effect on your life—it is, after all,
just a scene you are observing, one that
involves water, caution, and large objects,
some of them moving, some of them not—
it is conceivable that you will want to add
today's viewing to the list of observations
you have been compiling lately. For example:

Time is moving faster than it used to, isn't it?
A love you did not think that you deserve
has come your way, and now you fear its loss
Whoever is running this place has a cruel streak
(very cruel). Children grow up and other than
offering advice over the telephone, you can't do much
about the chances they will take with their lives
Besides, you've taken some chances of your own

And yes, that's the telephone ringing right now
After you hang up—maybe later, when you're
in bed—don't be surprised if you can't sleep:
you're not the only one who's up at this hour
thinking about that great vessel out there on

the water, restraining itself from getting
anywhere near Port Elizabeth, New Jersey
in order not to inflict any unintentional damage
upon itself, or worse, upon nature and its progeny

And so it goes. Every night, all over the world,
the stars arrange themselves above the shipping channels
to see what lessons they can learn. And even whales,
who ply the dangerous deep, have been known to
sing songs about the kind of life and death dramas they
have observed taking place so amazingly close to shore

Here You Are

Here you are: in a car, in a steady rain, on a country road
        halfway between a town
that is famous for the art of conversation and a dinner party
        where there will be more of the same
But why not? What else? These are, in fact, the things
        we do: we visit each other
Sometimes we purchase goods and services, clean house,
        labor over necessary tasks, cook food

while halfway around the world (well, those are just words:
        the real distance is unimaginable)
there is a place where a strange face has been carved
        into an ancient rock
The face is just a circle, a nimbus seemingly arising
        from a stalk of light
You may have seen this picture in a magazine or,
        more likely, in a dream

which makes you wonder: is there a connection here
        that needs to be addressed?
Perhaps it's just that the rain keeps up all night
and you have gotten so drunk that you have to
        sleep on a couch in the country house
where you can't stop yourself from worrying
        about being surrounded by rising water

in much the same indescribable way you have begun
        to worry
that the rock-carved face arising from a stalk of light
        may have been created
(and it was, it is) for no other reason than
        to look across the world, at you

The Days of Joy

In the morning, on the bus, before the sun is even up,
one woman on her way to work is describing to another
the layout of her kitchen, which is inefficient
Everybody on the bus wonders: what can be done?
Perhaps, someone suggests, the builders were thinking
        of monuments instead of households

Meanwhile, a schoolboy disembarks and begins
his journey to the playing fields, where he gets the feeling
that he is being spied upon by ancient constellations—
fish, crabs, archers, twins—that once traded gossip
        about young kings and their chambermaids

Thus the suspicion arises among certain members
of the traveling public that we are all walking between
the footsteps of others. That some of the experiences
we remember with total clarity never really happened
        or else took place many ages ago

Which is why someone like you may suddenly stop
beside your closet door and try to remember
what year it was that you bought that velvet dress,
those silver shoes; what dream you thought you would
        be dressing for, what life, what days of joy

And perhaps you will remember, one evening on your travels
between the love nests of Byzantium and the ends of the world
that are visible only to those who have managed to open their
third eye, because you must have left them somewhere, the things
you need if there is any hope of undergoing your next scheduled
regeneration: the address. The key to the room. The note
        that reveals the time, the place, the secret

You Still Look Good in a Hat

No matter how much you want to avoid
being one of those people who remembers
too much, sometimes you just get taken by surprise,
like when the ghost of a rainy Sunday morning
pops up out of nowhere, unwraps a snack,
and makes itself comfortable on your couch

It says it used to know your parents
It says it wants a beer. It confesses
that it has been feeling unsettled lately,
a little depressed, maybe even crazy
Then it sings a song about a girl
walking down the lane in a park,
after which it turns on the radio and cries

Still, it's no surprise to find old friends
behaving like this because we've all been
struggling lately, trying to figure out
how old we are in terms of how we feel—
always a mistake since certainly, we are
in the pre-diagnosis phase of *something*:

the heart flutters at three a.m.
Sparrows on the lawn look like
they are ready to break the kind of news
that no one ever wants to hear

And yet, there is the occasional compensation:
Perhaps your visitor, after trying on all
your clothes and complaining that baseball
isn't what it used to be, will grudgingly cough up
a photograph it has been carrying around for years,

the one that shows you mooning around
the back bedroom of that grim little house

you used to live in and thinking—based on
no evidence at all—that you were something special

Well lucky you: at last, the proof has turned up!
And now, people who hardly even know you are
beginning to talk about how good you still look in a hat

In Kitty Kat Dresses

There it is: the future
showing its claws to the girls
in kitty-kat dresses and the boys
with bad intentions

It looms over the continent
never even stopping
to buy refreshments or
take a nap on someone's couch

So watch out, Children of Tomorrow:
the future has met the aliens
and it doesn't care where they are from,
nor does it care where we are going

but it's coming with us
bringing nothing but its own
blind and insatiable determination
to see this thing through

You are the Blonde at the Party

If it matters, then yes, you are beautiful
You are the blonde at the party
with the far-away look in her eye
The night is your secret,
which is why it follows you around,
why the stars form a message
that the Egyptians misinterpreted
(all those pyramids, those buried boats)
because it was meant only for you

And if it matters, then yes, we love you
We just didn't know how to express it
in the time of great darkness
when the elemental forces
were just beginning to assert themselves
and the creatures of the zodiac
were arguing about which house
to occupy. Forgive us; we were
consumed with becoming. We did
not know how much we did not know

So if it matters, then yes, we will try harder
to provide a sense of universal comfort
We will try harder to light the
unknowable way forward
that is unknowable even to us
Soon, we will come to your room
We will brush your hair and help you dress
and in the lamplight, as you select
your jewelry, we can talk about the things
that you would never mention at the party

Because what matters is
we know that you are frightened
but think about it: so are we

With an infinity of tricks and troubles
electrifying our thoughts, with
so much danger at our fingertips,
we've had to learn that we are
here to help. To be a little gentler
as we walk you to the door

In Her Other Life

In the dream she had last night,
black horses ran wild through the capital
            and she had let them loose
The wind climbed through her window
and confessed that it had sealed the fate
            of an ancient kingdom
Then it wept in her arms. The moon said
            that time is just a signal fire
marking the horizon for the setting sun

In the mood she's in today, she could see
            straight through love
She could wear a scarlet dress and pose
            under a yum-yum tree
She could cry havoc on the streets
            of the city,
say her prayers under an open sky

Tomorrow, it will rain and rain and rain
All the announcements will be made at
            distant stations
and though she will wish that she could
            hear them
she hopes that in her other life
she doesn't have to live and die by
            what's in the news

First with Splendor

On a stage in an auditorium
in a city where you may live,
a person you may know, who has had
either a near-death experience or
some other strange encounter,
is trying to explain why we are not
who we think we are. Or what
For example, the speaker says,

it has become clear to him that the brain
is not the master of the self as has
long been claimed. In fact, the brain
can best be likened to an electrical storm:
impressive but unstable. True, it watches
TV for us, explains how to board trains
and write a grocery list, but it also longs
to lurk around the corners of our friends'
apartments because it wonders why
they are doing so much better than we are
or why they are doing worse, in which case,
it will send some sort of greeting card

That leaves us with the question of the mind,
which therefore must exist not in a labyrinth
of jealous cells but rather in some compartment
of infinity that as yet prefers not to reveal itself
Let me show you, says the speaker on the stage
and then abruptly, falls through the floor
This, however, is only a reference to how people
all over the world have been undergoing the kind
of separation where all they know to do is kiss
and wave good-bye. Which is not to say

that we did not love each other first with
splendor and then with gratitude, in a way

that turned the blue evening of every day
into the mighty weapons that we still believe
we carry with us, and though these may in fact
exist or only be imagined, all over the world
they wield the power of this human love as we
recall it, here in this place, this life, this hour,
when the infinite heart does all the thinking
and all that it can think about is you

Magic City

It was in the bars and dance clubs of the magic city
that we formed the plans with which we began our lives:
the comedian, the beautiful wife, the actor, the boy and girl

How many ways can we explain why we don't visit anymore?
After all, everyone who was ill has luckily obtained
at least some kind of cure. And everyone still waves hello
Our homes are lit by love and candlelight, or were, or should
have been, someday, some night, somewhere along our travels

And still it seems there are so many ways in which
we have begun the process of putting things aside
Some more than others; each in a fashion of their own:

A kiss lingers
An old friend smiles to himself
just before he leaves the stage

Dreamland

When you look out the windows of this house
you can see the ocean. Clean the bedroom,
arrange the spoons, and there it is:
the great deep, growling at the shore
So how can it be avoided, the juxtaposition
of the household and the eternal? Not that
anyone really wants to think those thoughts,

especially on a visiting day when the
grown children will be arriving from the city
We will take them to "a quaint café," meaning,
someplace we can afford, and listen as they
discuss their jobs; the things they do, the
events and processes they are responsible for,
which they describe in words we can only

pretend to understand. They are smart and
vicious, these skilled combatants that we
have raised. They are new people for a new
world, and so we go on loving them, though
back at home we seek advice from the TV

What do you want? it asks us. From warehouses
in distant locations, many types of items can be
put into boxes and delivered straight to your door
While these may include music from your childhood

and pictures of the cities where your plans evolved,
don't be surprised if there are also several versions
of a guidebook for the dead. All of this—as you
have no doubt guessed—is how the modern age
suggests the infinite, infinitely repeating, wave
after wave. But then, it was your choice to buy
this house. *Is that what you had in mind?*

It's all right if you aren't sure, since no one is
But let's put that on the list of topics to be discussed,
oh, sometime soon. Meanwhile, we'll just have to
keep weighing our losses against our luck, and on

our better days, here at the edge of dreamland,
try to prepare for the next turn of events
which, while bearing us no personal malice,
is already making note of our address

The Story of Tomorrow

If what we have always suspected is true,
then the story of tomorrow
is being written by people we cannot see
except from the corners of our eyes
They are the ones who know when the moon
will fly away and the seas will empty
(Yes, the big things that go *boom!*),
which is also what the time travelers talk about
at their seminars: special breathing techniques
to practice when they visit the conflagration,
chakra exercises to overcome the effects of
total darkness, of endless, empty roads

But we are never mentioned (earthly rabble!)
Not in a document, not on a hologram or slide,
which means that we are going to be left
to fend for ourselves. So brothers, start writing
the manifestos and inscribe them on the stones
that line those roads: when we embark upon
the raging days, our smaller fates are coming with us
and they need to know how hard we tried
to plan for this, how little information we
were given, how long we labored to understand
(think *eons, epochs*) the hidden meaning that
some still believe can be uncovered in our lives

By Nine A.M. You Are Expected

By nine a.m. you are expected in mid-town
Manhattan (Chicago, Boise, Louisville,
Cleveland, Kiev). Everyone is expected
Already, in your office, the computers are
opening their own files and condemning you
The bosses are emerging from the
underground tombs where they prefer to sleep
and marching in rigid lockstep towards the city
Whichever city: the one they have sunk their teeth into
The one they wheel around from place to place
so you can't find it on the weekends,
when it is only available to celebrities

But today, it seems that you are late
Yes you: we see you out there on your porch,
watching the moon, which is itself
mooning around the morning sky, reluctant,
apparently, to take its leave according to the
posted schedule. And we can tell you are
enjoying this disorder, unlike the ancients,
who must have thought some terrible fate
was in the offing if even the kitchen gods
could not sweep away the items meant
to be used only for the overnight display

Yes, our boy, the moon. Round as a saucer
Often cited as comparable to a china plate
Happy, shining, smiling, and friend to all
who sit up after midnight worrying about
what tomorrow will bring. City by city,
this is how the next phase will begin:
with a retelling of events in which
we do not fear the wicked and are
at peace with the unknown. The days
and nights become our dear companions
and scour the sky equally with rain and
sunshine, just to prove they mean no harm

The Afterlife

Things seem to be separating, don't they,
            each from the other?
That is what is troubling the white swan who has
sought you out (you, specifically), after leaving
            the last page of some neglected fairytale
Finally finding you on the path to ___ (fill in
            where you were going, please)
he says, *I am beginning to believe that we
            are not really here*
Even though this message is enigmatic,
            you suspect that it is true

Has always been. And so it is getting harder
to do the job, to wash the shirts, to buy
            the daily bread
with lightning jabbing at your every step
and the gods of thunder lurking around the corners
            of your house on Itty Bitty Pity Street
(Perhaps that was your destination all along?)
You would think that they would just let you live
            (the gods, the swans; even electricity)
but that, as it turns out, is never the case

Now even the skulls hiding out in the back yard
say they are worried that secrets are being
            kept from them
But what can you do? This was the only place
left to rent after all the other spaces had been
            taken up, or so you were told
And you've already moved in your things, punched
            the obligatory holes in the wall

So you might as well bake up some
        blood and bone biscuits
and invite everyone over for a confab
        because it looks like
you are all in this together; because the minutes
        of the last meeting show
that tomorrow and tomorrow and tomorrow
was never really planning to be your friend

The Eye of Horus

Here it is: another day when you feel
like you are being watched by the Eye of Horus,
that double-hearted god more vicious
than anyone remembers. He is lurking
back there in time, holding a grudge

but not against you, specifically
So, as the Protector of the Roads, he will
let you pass, carrying all the freight you
have been charged with and destined—
or so it is assumed—to wander forever,

unless he bends the centuries
and permits you to camp in the place of
Coming into Being. All around,
you will hear the world murmuring,
wondering if these are its last hours

because every night, science suffers:
secretly, all living things worry that Dawn,
weighing the testimony of her heart against
the burden of events she will be forced to witness,
will decide to quit her job. That holy, vaporous girl:
if she isn't properly rewarded, she may refuse us all

But distances will crumble anyway, then
soon rebuild themselves. Plagues will continue
to descend upon the houses of the poor
and lights go on and off without a reason
So if you want, you can give her nothing,

especially now, under these conditions,
in a time when staying human may be
the only way to answer the question of
how hard it is, really, to see in the dark

72

The Crab Nebula

Expecting just another day, the dresser
provides clothes, breakfast hums along
The morning begins to discuss its usual
            transportation issues
and tries to find the many things it needs

Outside however, the moon looms large
It hangs over the middle of the street
            as if it, too, is waiting for a bus
It may want a ride, or it may be thinking
            about calling back the tides
just to satisfy a need for catastrophe, which
            it has been known to do before,
although this news has generally been suppressed

But you, oh happy heart! Oh faithful
            little automaton!
You wouldn't even know it if the world
            had ended
You'd still be standing at the bus stop
            waiting for the N15
and wondering why the Crab Nebula
(the one with the beady eyes and
            bad intentions)
was suddenly taking such an interest in you

Suburban Byways

Of all the things we want (and we have a list;
      probably you do, too),
the most important is to be spirited away
      to someplace safe
Oh, if only the removing men would come!
Big men with sweetheart faces who know
      exactly where to go
Or just give us the directions and we will
      get there ourselves
We will cross the witch's forest, the chilly lake
      "where dwells a monster"
We have outwitted (read: *charmed* or *murdered*)
      many others like this before

And in the next place, let all the colors be minty!
(What terrible tales can be told, bad outcomes
      arise among pastels?)
Only one sun in the sky, one evil planet
      beaming poison rays
For that, we can deploy the astrological remedies
we were led to be believe would be just the ticket
      when worlds collide

And let us have an animal: a big one, with wings,
      who will patrol the roads
and pose those antique riddles to the souls
who wander suburban byways carrying
      the mixing bowls of human events
Today, those vessels seem to present
      no burden
Tomorrow—well, you don't want to know

So join us. Sign this petition
Undo whatever spell you used
      to weaponize your heart

Help us to find what rumor says may be
the last method of escape: the lamplit house,
            the summer evening,
the woman sitting at an open window
            still dreaming
that something wonderful will guide her fate

Time Sits Heavily

In the middle of the night, it becomes apparent
that your brain is leaking. This is a symptom, surely,
but not the first. After all, there are no additions anymore
Everything is a subtraction, a great loss. But you
won't tell anyone that this is what it feels like now
Not yet. Not while you are still pretending to be a
charmer, a sweetie pie. An up-to-date and modern girl

But how much longer, really, can you keep this up?
In a dark, square room at the end of the line
a bloody omen puts on a hat you used to wear and
screams bloody murder. As a famous study written with
the support of outside funding explains, this can only be
described as an ex-barrel of laughs, and you, my friend,
are an ex-participant. Thus, what else can be concluded
but that there are only so many messages left to convey?

And here's a big one: more than you think remains
a mystery, and with good reason—probably—
will never be explained. Though yes, of course,
in the empty house, "time sits heavily" on the couch
beside you, looking swollen and dumb. It barks out
its claim that it never really liked you anyway, and refuses
to let you pet it anymore. But why should you grieve
at this point in the drama, when what you need to do
is mark your paper according to what's obvious:
that modernity was never anything more than a
literature course, and all the girls that you relied on,
even those in silver boots who rode in on silver
horses, have long since grown up and gone away

Hence, when you reach the line of demarcation—
and that's the beauty of this trick—you are not only
free to choose your poison but also free to go
Which is what it really feels like when you think

about it (and you will), when the ghosts look up
from their eternal knitting to demand an answer
to the question, *friend or foe?* And at last,
you will know what to tell them: that you
still have the strength, the pure desire
to make that decision all by yourself

The Girl of the Lonely Horizons

She wakes up at dusk
in a house that does not know her
Not a chair will befriend her,
not a door will open or close
in response to her desires
So this is what it is like, she thinks
meaning, to be alone in a land of
flat fields, flat horizons
that are waiting to express
whatever is indicated by their
creator, who at the moment,
appears to have gone silent
Perhaps He is away

Sitting on a bed, looking out a
window, in a pose that references
a previously undetected Order of Things,
she reviews the little information that
she has: her name, her age,
which she will eventually be required
to provide, but only after
the rivers run, the wheels turn,
the seasons form and fade, automatically
If the planets have any influence
on these matters, they are
keeping it to themselves

So with nothing else to do
(which is where the theory of
random choice begins to give her
some ideas), she wanders through the rooms
and finds a bureau full of stars,
leftovers, probably, that can be
used to fill in empty spaces
It's infuriating, really, she thinks,
how little they tell us about these things

Soon, the night puts up its dark glass walls,
as it has done before, as it will do again
Downstairs, the Pillars of Creation
are gathering the energy they need—
the scarves of light and gases—
to burp out universes, launch enigmas,
bend and sweep and scatter celestial matter
all the way back to the beginning of time,
and forwards,

towards the shore of some infinite dawning,
which is where she was headed, anyway,
our girl of the lonely horizons,
who thinks that she has been underestimated,
who has come prepared with a few tricks of her own
So it is no surprise
when she raises the narrow viewing tube of the future

and sees a laborer in a sun-god suit
hauling a golden cart across the equinox
It will take him ages, eons, to get where he is going
but she is ready to bet
that just the right quirk of human nature
will be enough
to stop this whole circus in its tracks

A Raincoat's Embrace

Well, you knew this had to happen:
that you would sit up in bed one night, thinking,
I feel like I have already left this world
And maybe you have. Or maybe not. In this life,
       so little is revealed

But if you stand at the window long enough,
you can watch the bad hours peel themselves
back from the horizon and fly away, as if
       no one needs them anymore
In other houses, lights go on. Children are
       awakened. Coffee is poured

In your house, the embrace of a raincoat
       brings back memories
An unexpected kiss finally explains itself
and you agree (we all agree) to soldier on

Little Girl, Little Boy

What you will find, little girl, little boy,
is that after the storm, there is only
one path, and it leads to the mill
at the end of the winding river
that grinds out the fate of the world
You can hear its groaning gears
all your life without reading, anywhere,
about a wounded machine that is
swallowing the stars. But doesn't
the sky look darker every night?
Isn't there a small bear missing from
the heavens? A bull? A great bird?
No one knows where the river begins
or why the mill is tireless, insatiable
You will be sent there anyway, with
many instructions, and though none of
them will be helpful, don't give up yet
People have been thinking about this
problem since they first opened their
eyes, which may have been yesterday
Or maybe, tomorrow

Evolution

Usually, the central authority issues some encouraging
phrase to start the day. (Remember, *Go get 'em, girls!*
That was a good one.) But today, the channel has
gone silent. Instead, the only news is that the
natural world has sent out a warning to everything
that is struggling to evolve. At your house, even the
potted plants are looking worried. And they are looking
        straight at you

So the chances are this could be death or just another kind
of trouble, but you won't know that for some time, not until
the warm days come to visit, opening windows and murmuring
endearments. You should lie down in summer's arms for a while
and try to remember what it feels like to be good
        and to be loved

Which perhaps is a suggestion that there may be other
options, other hopes. After all, just in the time when you
were struggling for each breath even though each breath
could be a punishment, blossoms have begun appearing
on the windowsill and something new and wonderful has
        quietly succeeded in being born

Dog Years

Look, I'm sure you knew how the story was
supposed to go, but didn't believe it. No one
who comes from the kind of place where we did
is that nice—or stupid. Meat on a plate was
never going to be served in restaurants, but run
to ground in some evil alley that would later be
the scene of all performances, paid and otherwise,
until such time as we wised up, which was always
        going to take years and years

And since it's clear that nothing will be given,
now comes the time to track down what can be
saved. You'll need a dog and a map of the stars,
neither of which will be found in any place that you
think to look, so think harder. Think like you live
in the underbelly, like no one knows you anymore,
        but still, you can't be stopped

Except, stop here, just for a moment: where there
is summer. Where there is this scene, composed
of fireflies, children, wet bathing suits on the porch
Yes, that house, where you did not live, which
was not yours, though something else was. Is.
Invisible and hungry. *Lost, lost, lost,* it says,
        and bares its teeth

But now it approaches you with an offer, fond
as it is of any woman who rescues a dog (did you
understand that was the clue?) So sit a while,
with your animal, at the edge of the family group
in the hour that is suspended between then and now,
when the lights are coming on, the food is cooking,
the moon rising, and you are permitted to
        remember everything

Which you do. And then, when the stars appear,
continue on your way. Headed where?
That would be, wherever you are expected:
down the road, into or out of darkness
Certainly, though the distance may be
measured not in light but dog years,
the clues—as you have seen—are everywhere
All you have to do is follow them: the time
          was always meant to be now

About the Author

Eleanor Lerman is a writer who lives in New York. Her first book of poetry, *Armed Love* (Wesleyan University Press, 1973), published when she was twenty-one, was nominated for a National Book Award. She has since published several other award-winning collections of poetry—*Come the Sweet By and By* (University of Massachusetts Press, 1975); *The Mystery of Meteors* (Sarabande Books, 2001); *Our Post-Soviet History Unfolds* (Sarabande Books, 2005); and *The Sensual World Re-Emerges* (Sarabande Books, 2010), along with *The Blonde on the Train* (Mayapple Press, 2009) a collection of short stories. She was awarded the 2006 Lenore Marshall Poetry Prize from the Academy of American Poets and the Nation magazine for the year's most outstanding book of poetry for *Our Post-Soviet History Unfolds* and received a 2007 Poetry Fellowship from the National Endowment for the Arts. In 2011 she received a Guggenheim Fellowship. Her first novel, *Janet Planet*, based on the life of Carlos Castaneda, was published by Mayapple Press in 2011.

Other Recent Titles from Mayapple Press:

Sally Rosen Kindred, *Book of Asters*, 2014
      Paper, 62pp, $14.95 plus s&h
      ISBN 978-1-936419-34-0

Stephen Lewandowski, *Under Foot*, 2014
      Paper, 80pp, $15.95 plus s&h
      ISBN 978-1-936419-32-6

Hilma Contreras (Judith Kerman, trans.), *Between Two Silences / Entre Dos Silencios*, 2014
      Paper, 122pp, $16.95 plus s&h
      ISBN 978-1-936419-31-9

Helen Ruggieri & Linda Underhill, Eds., *Written On Water: Writings About the Allegheny River*, 2013 (Includes Bonus CD!)
      Paper, 90pp, $19.95 plus s&h
      ISBN 978-1-936419-30-2

Don Cellini, *Candidates for sainthood and other sinners / Aprendices de santo y otros pecadores*, 2013
      Paper, 62pp, $14.95 plus s&h
      ISBN 978-1-936419-29-6

Gerry LaFemina, *Notes for the Novice Ventriloquist*, 2013
      Paper, 78pp, $15.95 plus s&h
      ISBN 978-1-936419-28-9

Robert Haight, *Feeding Wild Birds*, 2013
      Paper, 82pp, $15.95 plus s&h
      ISBN 978-1-936419-27-2

Pamela Miller, *Miss Unthinkable*, 2013
      Paper, 58pp, $14.95 plus s&h
      ISBN 978-1-936419-26-5

Penelope Scambly Schott, *Lillie was a goddess, Lillie was a whore*, 2013
      Paper, 90pp, $15.95 plus s&h
      ISBN 978-1-936419-25-8

Nola Garrett, *The Pastor's Wife Considers Pinball*, 2013
      Paper, 74pp, $14.95 plus s&h
      ISBN 978-1-936419-16-6

Marjorie Manwaring, *Search for a Velvet-Lined Cape*, 2013
      Paper, 94pp, $15.95 plus s&h
      ISBN 978-1-936419-15-9

Edythe Haendel Schwartz, *A Palette of Leaves*, 2012
      Paper, 74pp, $14.95 plus s&h
      ISBN 978-1-936419-14-2

For a complete catalog of Mayapple Press publications, please visit our website at *www.mayapplepress.com*. Books can be ordered direct from our website with secure on-line payment using PayPal, or by mail (check or money order). Or order through your local bookseller.